AF270376

# VANS

# VANS

KENNY ABDO

Fly!
An Imprint of Abdo Zoom
abdobooks.com

**abdobooks.com**

Published by Abdo Zoom, a division of ABDO, P.O. Box 398166, Minneapolis, Minnesota 55439. Copyright © 2025 by Abdo Consulting Group, Inc. International copyrights reserved in all countries. No part of this book may be reproduced in any form without written permission from the publisher. Fly!™ is a trademark and logo of Abdo Zoom.

Printed in the United States of America, North Mankato, Minnesota.
102024
012025

Photo Credits: Alamy, Getty Images, Shutterstock
Production Contributors: Kenny Abdo, Jennie Forsberg, Grace Hansen
Design Contributors: Candice Keimig, Neil Klinepier, Laura Graphenteen

**Library of Congress Control Number: 2024936545**

**Publisher's Cataloging-in-Publication Data**

Names: Abdo, Kenny, author.
Title: Vans / by Kenny Abdo
Description: Minneapolis, Minnesota : Abdo Zoom, 2025 | Series: Sneakerheads |
    Includes online resources and index.
Identifiers: ISBN 9781098287481 (lib. bdg.) | ISBN 9781098288181 (ebook) |
    ISBN 9781098288532 (Read-to-me ebook)
Subjects: LCSH: Sneakers--Juvenile literature. | Shoes--Juvenile literature. |
    Fashion--Social aspects--Juvenile literature. | VF Corporation--Juvenile
    literature.
Classification: DDC 391.413--dc23

# TABLE OF CONTENTS

# VANS

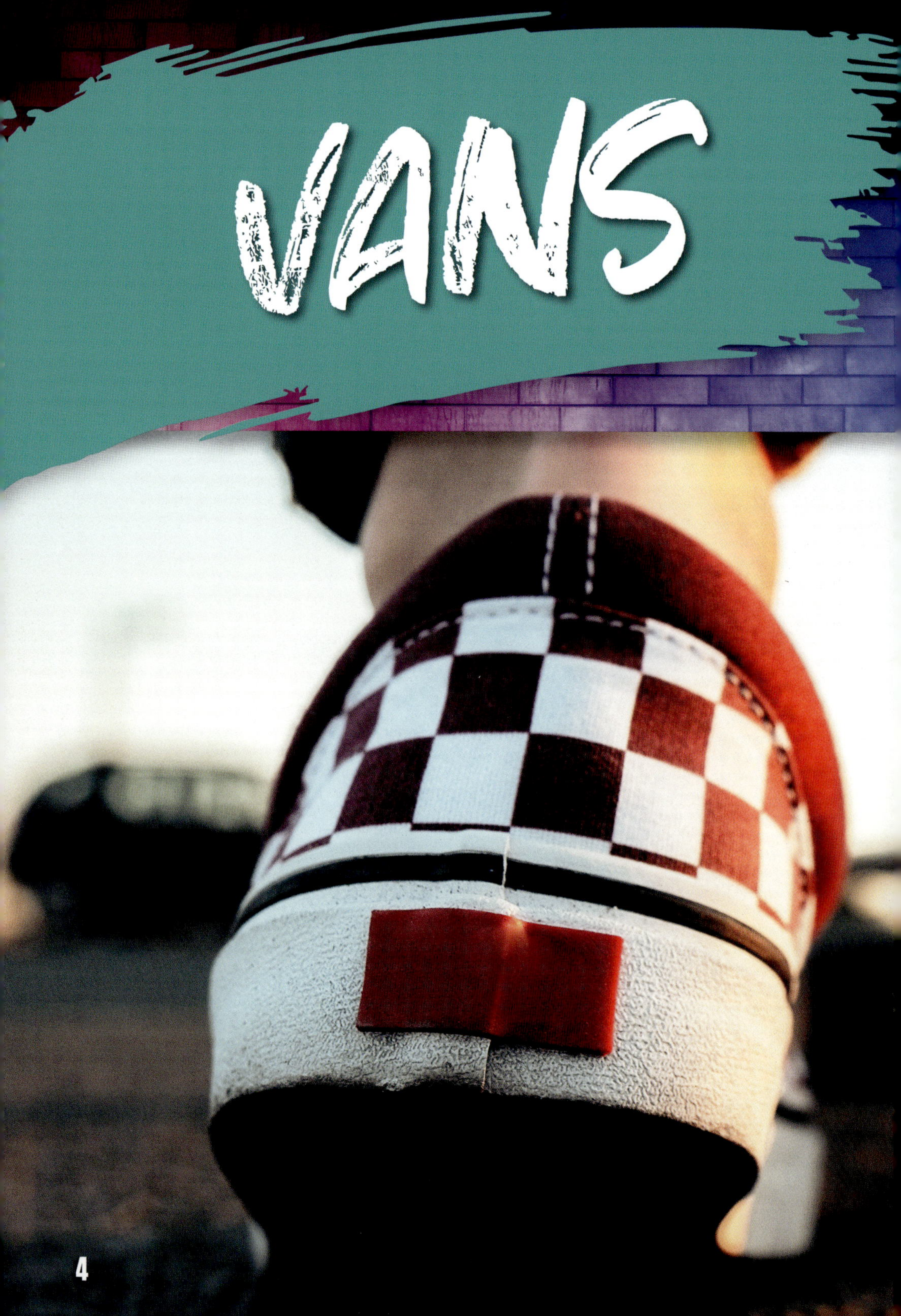

With its start as a small **made-to-order** shoe shop, Vans quickly skated past the rest of the sneaker **brands** of the world!

Over the decades, Vans has gone from creating simple low-top shoes to becoming an iconic **brand** among skateboarders, surfers, and sneakerheads!

# THE OGs

Brothers Paul and Jim Van Doren had an idea. They wanted to make shoes for the locals in their hometown, Anaheim, California. But they would sell the shoes directly to customers, not to **retailers**.

The brothers and their business partners finally achieved their dream. The Van Doren Rubber Company opened its doors in 1966. The name was shortened to House of Vans soon after.

# THE KICKS

Located in Southern California, the shop was in the right place at the right time. Two of the first big names to wear the shoes were skateboarders Tony Alva and Stacey Peralta.

Alva and Peralta wore the original style #44 shoe. They added padding to the **collar** with other small changes. The shoe became the style #95. Eventually, it was renamed the Era. The shoe was the first skate shoe designed by skateboarders.

HALF
CAB™
©1992VANS®
HALF
CAB
©1992VANS®

Business boomed over the next decade. By the end of the 1970s, Vans had **debuted** the Old Skool, Classic Slip-On, and Sk8-Hi. These sneakers could be customized so skaters could express themselves.

In 1982, the Vans Slip-Ons made their **big screen debut**. The shoes were featured in the hit comedy *Fast Times at Ridgemont High*. Actor Sean Penn requested that his character wear them. This gave the **brand** worldwide attention, **skyrocketing** sales.

In 1996, Vans began its **sponsorship** of the Warped Tour. Vans fused music, skateboarding, and shoes for the event. The Vans Warped Tour became the longest-running concert series in America.

VANS
Customs
22
EASILY CREATE A UNIQUE PAIR WITH YOUR PHOTOS
1 UPLOAD A FAVORITE PHOTO YOU TOOK
2 POSITION YOUR IMAGE TO MAKE IT JUST RIGHT
3 FINISH YOUR DESIGN AND MAKE THEM YOURS

Vans launched Vans Customs in 2004. It allowed anyone to create their own Classic Slip-Ons. Sneakerheads could use hundreds of different color and pattern combinations!

After 1992, Vans did not release any new designs. In 2016, the company began **collaborating** with major fashion designers. From KITH to Supreme to Kenzo, each company put its own spin on the shoes!

# THE RESTOCK

Vans went viral on the internet in 2016. In it, a kid admires a friend's pair of Vans. Sales **skyrocketed**! Someone sold a pair of the same shoes, claiming they were from the video. They went for more than $400,000. Sadly, they were fake.

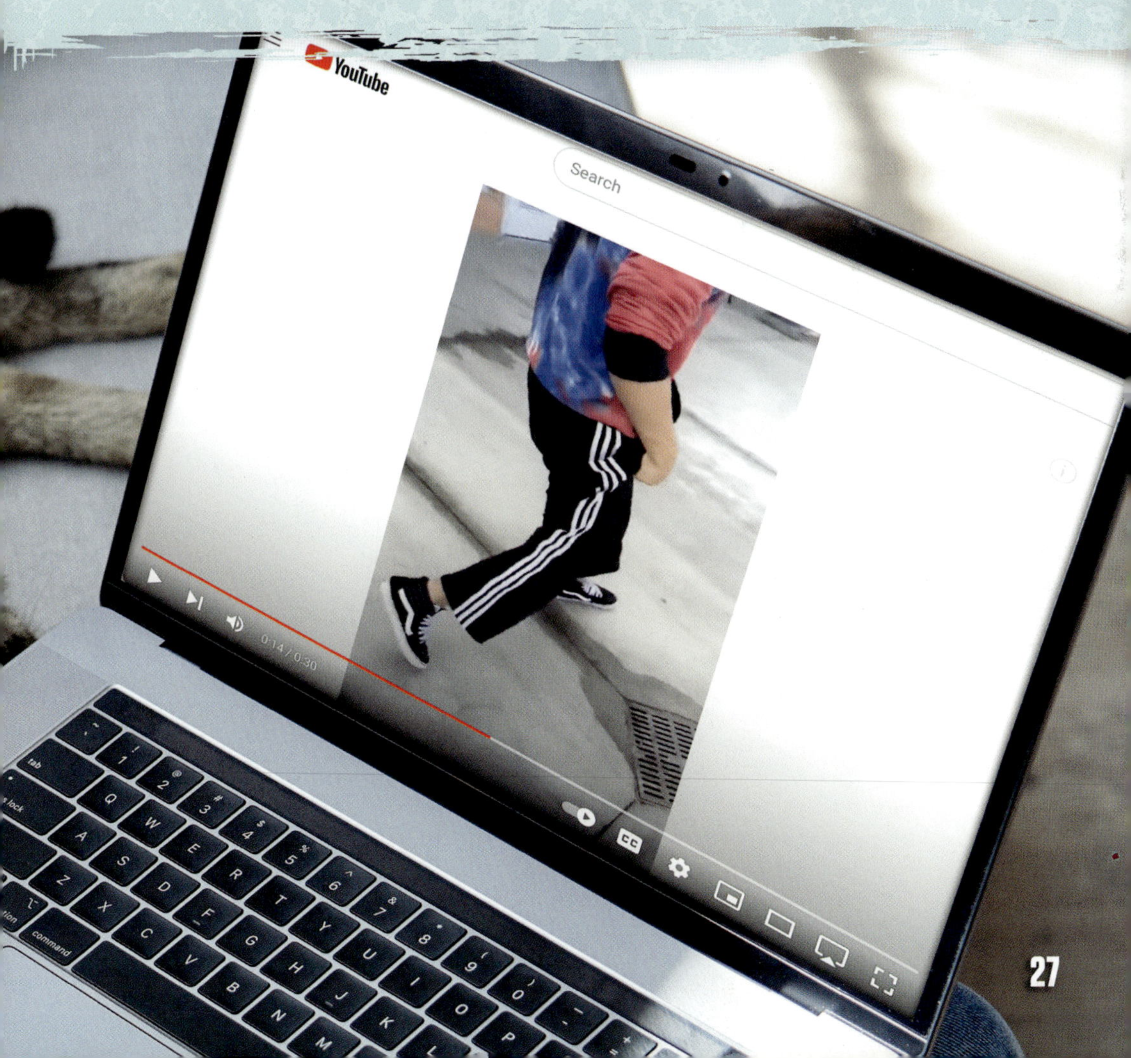

VANS

The Van Doren brothers wanted to take a simple design and bring it straight to the people. Instead, Vans slipped into pop culture history!

# GLOSSARY

**big screen** – another name for the movies.

**brand** – a name, design, or symbol that separates one product from another.

**collaborate** – to work with another person or group to do something or reach a goal.

**collar** – the top edge of a shoe where the foot is inserted.

**debut** – a first appearance.

**made-to-order** – specially made according to a customer's specifications.

**retailer** – a company that sells goods to the public in stores and on the internet.

**skyrocket** – to rise or cause to rise with the speed, suddenness, and height of a rocket.

**sponsorship** – money that is given, usually by a company, to support a person, organization or activity.

# ONLINE RESOURCES

**Booklinks**
**NONFICTION NETWORK**
FREE! ONLINE NONFICTION RESOURCES

To learn more about Vans, please visit **abdobooklinks.com** or scan this QR code. These links are routinely monitored and updated to provide the most current information available.

# INDEX